SOLAR ENERGY

SOLAR ENERGY

JOHN HOKE

AN !MPACT BOOK
FRANKLIN WATTS
NEW YORK | LONDON
1978
REVISED EDITION

FRONTISPIECE: A SOLAR ECLIPSE

Photographs courtesy of:
Yerkes Observatory: frontispiece; John Hoke: pp. 3, 12, 16, 24, 27, 33, 47, 48, 53, 56 (bottom), 59 (top and bottom), 62, 63, 65 (top and bottom), 68, 70, 73, 75, 76; Smithsonian Institution: p. 4; NASA: pp. 7, 20, 40, 43; University of Delaware: p. 28; Edmund Scientific Co.: p. 56 (top).

Library of Congress Cataloging in Publication Data

Hoke, John, 1925–
    Solar energy.

    (An Impact book)
    Bibliography: p.
    Includes index.
    SUMMARY: Discusses and describes solar cells, techniques for using solar energy, solar heating of a house, and possible future uses of solar energy. Includes school projects and a materials list.
    1.   Solar energy—Juvenile literature.   [1. Solar energy.   2.   Experiments]
TJ810.H6   1978   621.47   77–16828
ISBN 0–531–01329–4

CONTENTS

THE SUN OF SUNS

The daily arrival of sunlight is vital to all life, for with sunlight comes the flood of energy that supports the growth of plants. And plantlife is the beginning—the source of food. Yet we take the sun for granted, and most of us seem unaware of the huge amount of energy it puts into our ecological system.

The energy of the sun feeds and clothes us, brings us the water we drink and is responsible for the many kinds of power we use to run our household equipment, our transportation, and our industry. For example all our hydroelectric power is derived originally from the sun. Seawater, evaporated by the sun, rises into the air, then falls upon the land—as rain or snow—to fill our rivers and reservoirs. And the force of water, running downhill back to the sea, provides much of the electric power we now use in our homes and cities and in industry.

Yet all this is only a fraction of the solar energy waiting to be put to work. If we were able to harness all the energy contained in several days' sunlight, covering an area the size of lake Erie, it would equal all the energy in all the fuels humans have burned on earth throughout time—as well as the energy in all the fossil fuels still underground!

Now, as populations increase, the use of power also increases. Yet the supply of fossil fuels is dwindling. New sources

(1)

of power must be found and scientists are looking to the sun as the most promising and the only unlimited source of future energy.

In fact, the natural process by which solar energy is converted to food and material for clothing and fuel is not very efficient. There is an enormous amount of waste; it takes aeons to make coal and oil.

The ways people have commonly put solar energy to use are not very efficient either. Planting crops, building dikes, and irrigating land take advantage of the sun's energy, but, again, much is wasted. The same amount of sunlight would do much more work if we could efficiently harness it.

Early uses of solar energy | Some ways of harnessing solar energy were discovered long ago. It has been said that centuries ago the Greek mathematician Archimedes used sunlight concentrated by many large reflectors to set fire to invading Roman ships. Early scientists knew that very intense heat could be generated by using sunlight. In 1772 the French scientist Antoine Lavoisier built a solar furnace hot enough to melt a number of metals. His concentrator was a huge lens that focused sunlight into a small area. With it he was able to conduct many chemical experiments needing high temperatures which only sunlight could then provide.

Other later experiments used large, dish-shaped **parabolic reflectors** to concentrate sunlight to run mechanical engines. Unfortunately, reflectors have to be aligned with the sun, are complicated, and work only when the sun is bright. Other systems, that did not have to be aligned with the sun, fared better. In Chile a huge water desalting system worked well for almost forty years. Ocean water was pumped into troughs. Sunlight, shining through panes of glass, evaporated the water which condensed as fresh water on the panes of glass. It then ran down the panes and collected in run-off troughs.

Solar recording of solar-caused surf.

The demand for constant power | But, as promising as early solar-power systems were, they did not offer power on demand. If we were to rely completely on solar energy what would we do about our needs at night, when there is no sun? Or during bad weather? Modern industrial society focused most of its attention on ways to have power on demand—at the flick of a switch. Fueled engines were inexpensive and burned fuels that were then cheap and plentiful.

However, the dawn of the space age revived our interest in solar energy.

This wooden model of the ancient south-pointing Chinese carriage is in the Smithsonian Institution. See page 68 for a modern version that is run on solar energy.

SOLAR ENERGY IN SPACE

When we first learned to put satellites—and astronauts—into orbit around the earth, the space age was born. At this time, early in the 1960s, the need to find a way to power spacecraft became intense. It is costly to put an object into space. To justify the cost, a satellite would have to function over a long period of time. It would need a continuous source of electric power. Without such a source of power, future space activities would be limited. Probes of many years—to other planets and beyond—would be impossible. While highly sophisticated batteries and power systems were available, they were all limited in one important way. As they provided electricity, they progressively exhausted themselves. And for the small amount of power they could supply, they were costly and heavy. What was needed was a power supply whose source of energy would be plentiful, continuous, and near at hand, no matter where the spacecraft went. The sun's energy was the only practical candidate for the job.

While other technology had been steadily improving over the years, solar-energy technology had not. Few devices born of earlier solar technology were of much use. Solar-heated machines

A full-scale mock-up of Surveyor spacecraft.
Note solar cells raised above it.

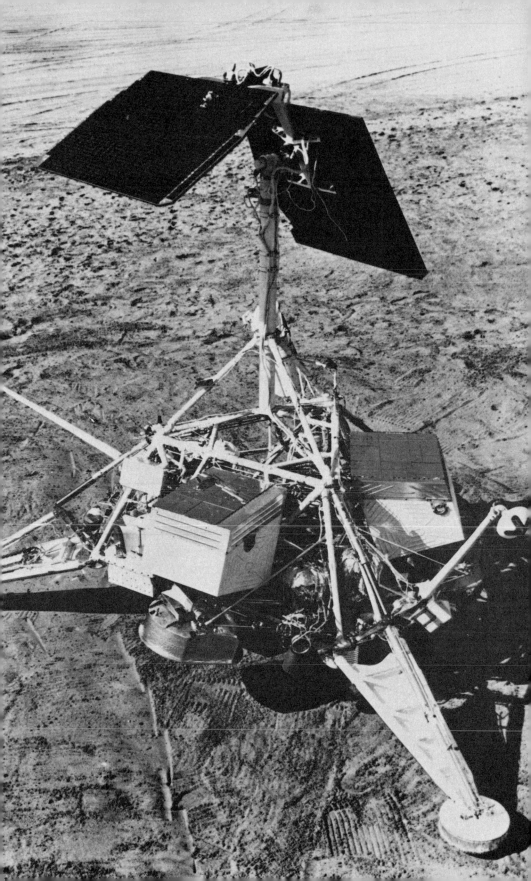

such as steam engines or hot-air engines or machines for heating or evaporating water were not useful for space. Among other things, they required periodic maintenance. Once an unmanned space probe was on its way, no one would be able to oil it or fix it periodically. A system was needed that could produce a continuous supply of electricity—enough to operate, without maintenance, all the equipment of any device put into space.

Actually, such an electric system had been in existence for a long time, although its function as a generator had not been given a great deal of attention.

THE PHOTOVOLTAIC CELL

As early as a century ago, it was known that certain materials would produce electrical energy when exposed to light. Late in the 1800s, an American named Charles Fritts developed the forerunner of the modern **photoelectric** cell. It was probably the first **photovoltaic** device. It is interesting that the major use of these cells was in light meters—instruments used by photographers for measuring the strength of light. The cells were not then used as power-generating devices, for at that time there were almost no machines or motors that could operate well on the limited amount of current they put out.

However, the unique way a photoelectric cell produces electricity attracted the attention of scientists. The cell creates electricity whenever light is falling on its photosensitive (light sensitive) surface. Moreover, there is no waste or breakdown of the material itself as a result of the process. While the actual output of power was at first so small as to be almost useless, scientists reasoned that the method probably could be made to work better. They knew that the amount of energy contained in sunlight was considerable. They also knew that a given amount of sunlight would be much stronger in nearby space than at earth level. On earth, we receive only what is left over after light has passed through the atmosphere, where a great deal of the original sunlight is reflected back into space or turned into heat.

For the space program, it seemed worthwhile to try to improve this method of converting light directly into electrical energy, and so, serious research efforts were begun.

THE SILICON SOLAR CELL

In 1954, the Bell Telephone Laboratories began making **solar cells** whose electrical output was many times greater than the inefficient cells that had been used in photographic light meters for so many years. The ability of these new cells to convert sunlight directly into electricity would, in time, approach the efficiency of some of the best of modern steam and gas engines. And, having no moving parts to wear out, the solar cells would not break down after long use. Finally, if built well, they would not need maintenance. They would produce electricity in usable amounts as long as light shone upon them. From a practical point of view, these new solar "batteries" were ideally suited to provide for the long-range electrical needs of future space satellites and manned spacecraft.

How a solar cell works | Modern solar cells are made of one of the earth's most common ingredients—silicon. But unlike other common forms of silicon, such as sand, the silicon used to make solar cells is very carefully prepared. (See page 10). An internal layer is created in the cell. This acts as a barrier to the movement of free electrons when they attempt to go in a particular direction. A flow of electricity takes place when the solar cell is exposed to light, and electron activity in its molecules is stimulated. In effect, the silicon barrier controls the direction of the flow. In addition, the chemical makeup of the silicon is so arranged that there is a higher percentage of electrons per molecule on the side of the barrier that will be exposed to light. The barrier layer allows electrons to flow through it in one direction only—in this case away from the light. So the electricity produced when light falls upon the cell is forced to move in a planned direction.

The silicon solar cell is made of a stable glasslike material, but one whose electron structure is planned to be in an uneasy state of balance. In the presence of light, the units of light—called

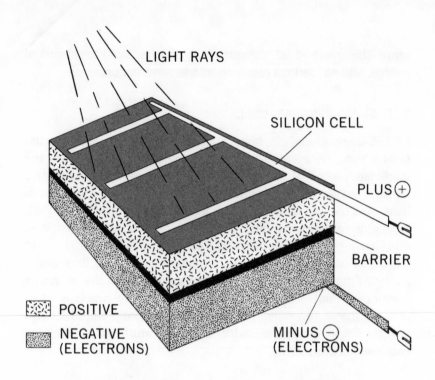

LIGHT RAYS

SILICON CELL

PLUS ⊕

BARRIER

POSITIVE

NEGATIVE
(ELECTRONS)

MINUS ⊖
(ELECTRONS)

**A cross-section of the silicon cell shows the
process for converting light to electricity.
(Some cells are made with the polarity reversed.)**

photons—are absorbed in the surface of the silicon where they
displace electrons. These electrons, no longer bound by their
parent molecules, move freely about. The barrier layer allows
these electrons to pass to the other side of the cell, but the
positive charges they leave behind cannot easily pass the barrier.
The result is that one side of the solar cell soon becomes saturated with the negatively charged electrons, while the other side
is saturated with positively charged "holes." In the normal state
of a material, all electrons are in place within each molecular
unit. So the electrons which have been freed and isolated from
their normal positions, now actively seek new positions in the
molecular structure of the cell. But they are separated by the
barrier from the holes into which they would ordinarily move.
Consequently, the only way the electrons and holes can easily

make contact is through some external path. And in providing the path—or circuit—we can harness this source of power.

The solar cell thus behaves very much like a battery having a negative and positive side: it will provide a flow of electrical current when it is hooked into a circuit. Like a battery, the solar cell can be equipped with a wire "lead" from each of its two sides. If the wires are connected, the result is a path for the electrons on one side of the cell to reach the positive charges on the other side. If the wires are hooked into the circuit in a piece of electrical equipment, the electron flow through this path will produce the current needed to operate the equipment.

Solar cells produce electricity in specific amounts under given light conditions. In general, they put out about half a volt under strong sunlight at the surface of the earth. The amount of current they produce depends upon how efficient they are. Some cells may be better current producers than others. After a batch has been made, individual solar cells are graded in terms of their percentage of **efficiency.** When the cells are used to make up a solar power supply for a piece of electrical equipment, cells of the same efficiency are used so that a uniform performance can be expected from the finished solar power supply. Also, the larger a solar cell is made, the more current it produces at half a volt. Because different kinds of electrical equipment require different amounts of **current** at different **voltages,** cells must be selected that will meet the proper voltage and current needs of the particular equipment.

**The silicon solar cell converts light directly
into electrical energy for an indefinite
period and without wearing out in any way.**

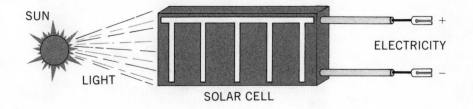

SUN

LIGHT

SOLAR CELL

ELECTRICITY

+

−

To get higher voltage, cells can
be "shingled" together in a series,
each cell adding about half a volt
to the string. This group puts
out about 2½ volts in full sunlight.

Modern solar cells are manufactured in a manner that makes it easy to hook them together in whatever combination of voltage and current output is required. The same is true of batteries used to operate an ordinary radio. A common flashlight battery puts out about 1½ volts with enough current to run the radio. If the radio needs 6 volts to operate, it takes four 1½-volt batteries. But if the radio draws a lot of current, bigger batteries must be used to provide the extra current. A very small radio may still need 6 volts but take less current to run. It can be operated with little penlight cells that provide less current but still put out the required voltage.

While solar cells, like batteries, are made so that they can be hooked up in many ways, they are usually soldered directly to each other so that their light-sensitive surfaces will all be facing in the same direction. Where the area available to put a solar cell generator is limited—on, say, a small satellite—solar cells are made in small squares, so that little or no wasted space exists between the cells. Square cells have often been put together by overlapping them, like roofing shingles—the back of one cell (the negative side) is on the top edge (positive side) of the next cell. The number of cells soldered together in a "shingle" series determines what the voltage output of the group will be. For example, if there are five solar cells in a shingled group, the combined assembly will deliver about 2½ volts in bright sunlight, and require only a small area for mounting the cells.

Thus, the voltage requirements of any particular job are met by putting as many cells as are needed into a long series— each small group of shingled cells being wired to other shingled groups, in a continuous series.

Unlike ordinary batteries, however, silicon solar cells are not available in a wide range of sizes. So, in a case where a single series of solar cells cannot provide enough current, additional identical strings of solar cells are hooked into a system known as a "parallel hookup." The number of parallel groups needed in a circuit depends on how much current is needed to operate a particular piece of equipment. If too few groups of cells in a series were used, the equipment would demand more current than the cells could provide. This would cause the overall voltage of the solar generator to drop so low that the equipment would fail to operate.

Great care is taken in preparing a solar power supply to do a given job. First of all, as soon as they are manufactured, the performance of a given batch of solar cells is measured. Their output in terms of voltage and current under given light conditions is also measured.

The user of solar cells then estimates the minimum amount of light that will be available, the voltage at which the equipment must operate, and how much current is needed to run it. With this information in hand, the cells are then combined. The right number of cells are soldered together in a series to meet voltage requirements. Then the proper number of these series-connected cells are wired, in parallel, to provide the current needed.

In most cases, all the prepared cells are cemented to a strong base material that keeps them firmly in place, with all cells facing in the same direction. Solar cells are very thin and as fragile as glass. A firm base serves both to protect them from breakage and to carry away excess heat absorbed by the cells when they are exposed to sunlight. As cells become hotter, they produce less and less power. So a means to absorb and remove heat is very important.

The finished solar panel will be located where sunlight will shine upon it. Once properly constructed, the solar panel can be expected to operate indefinitely—as long as light reaches it.

There is another factor that often has to be considered when designing a solar generator. Does the equipment it powers have to run only when there is light, or must it be able to operate at night as well? If the equipment must run at night, the solar panel will have to have an electrical output great enough to provide extra power that can be stored in rechargeable batteries. The batteries will then power the equipment during periods of darkness.

Fortunately, many excellent rechargeable batteries have been developed. While they do not last indefinitely—as do the solar cells—they can provide many years of service, sufficient for most space needs. Usually, a battery package is assembled that can power the equipment all the time, and the solar bank is used only to recharge these constantly draining batteries. The equipment itself gets all of its operating power from the bank of batteries—whether or not light is shining on the solar generator.

How solar cells are made | Though ideally suited as a power source for space needs, solar cells have one drawback as a common power source on earth. They are more expensive than conventional power supplies. Even though they could provide power indefinitely and efficiently from their "free" source, it would take many years' output of free energy to offset their high initial cost. For example, if you were to shingle a small part of your rooftop with enough solar cells able to provide for all your household electric power needs, the solar panel alone could cost many thousands of dollars—maybe several times the cost of your house. During your lifetime, you might not use anywhere near as many dollars' worth of power from conventional sources to do the same job.

Solar cells are costly because research is expensive and the process of manufacturing these cells is very complicated. It requires very careful chemical processing, delicate stonecutting and polishing, and intricate electrical circuitry. Simplified ways of making solar generators will probably be developed. But at present, making solar cells is like making jewelry. Costs have come down over the years, however. While one watt's worth of solar cells cost over two hundred dollars in the early 1960s, today the same amount costs less than thirty dollars.

Let us examine some of the steps involved in making these cells. The raw silicon is first purified until it has reached the cleanest state technically possible. A very precise measure of arsenic is added to this molten silicon. These steps are carried out in an enclosed furnace to make sure that nothing else gets into the "melt," as it is called, to spoil its purity.

From this melt, a single large crystal of the "doped" silicon is grown. This is a delicate process in which a single crystal ingot of silicon is formed. As it is slowly drawn from the melt, it solidifies. The finished ingot, which can be as large as a cucumber, is then sliced into very thin wafers.

**The author designed this solar boat.
Solar panels overhead and on
the prow charge the batteries
of this mobile power supply
convenient for remote areas.**

Because all these steps are necessary, and very expensive, great care is taken to cut as many slices as possible from the single ingot. When the solar cells are to be located in a limited area, the circular slices are trimmed by diamond-grit saws into squares or rectangles. The saw has a very thin blade, to keep down the waste. Even so, a lot of the material is lost in both cutting and trimming. In terrestrial (earthly) use of solar-cell generators, it is not so necessary to cover every square inch of area with solar cells. While round solar cells may take up more space, they are much less wasteful of material, since the slices do not have to be trimmed into squares.

After the wafers—square or round—have been cleaned, they are placed in rows on a flat tray. This tray is then put into a special furnace where boron vapor diffuses atoms of boron onto the surface of the silicon wafers. This is a critical process requiring that everything be kept exceptionally clean, because the slightest contamination from other materials can seriously harm the product. It is this process that creates the interior barrier layer which controls the flow of electrons through the finished cell—so important in the cell's ability to generate electricity efficiently.

Next, the boron-diffused cells are cleaned again. While silicon is one of the best materials for making solar cells, it is not easy to solder anything to it directly. To overcome this difficulty, a special tinning or plating process deposits a thin layer of metal solder on the cells. This base, though weak and easily pulled away from the cell, will make it possible to solder cells together.

After the cells have been plated—"tinned"—the excess solder is removed, and the cells are tested to see if they will perform properly. In this process, they are graded, and all cells of the same efficiency are kept together. In most cases, the completed solar panel's output is only as good as the least efficient cells in the system; so matching the cells in a panel is important. Naturally, high-efficiency cells are best for use in space. Their output will be higher in proportion to their weight and size. Cells that have lower efficiency but still yield reasonably high outputs are used for making solar panels where the area is not so limited.

Once all these steps have been carried out, the cells can perform their function indefinitely. But, as you can see, it is expensive to get the cells to this stage of development. In the future, technology should gradually improve so that costs of producing solar cells can be brought down. A current government research objective is to bring their cost down to fifty cents per watt. Until this happens, however, solar cells will rarely be used where cheaper sources of power are available.

SOLAR POWER FOR SPACE SATELLITES

In 1958, the VANGUARD I space satellite was placed in orbit. It was the first American satellite to use solar cells to generate electricity from sunlight in order to power a small transmitter. For many years, this satellite continued to broadcast. Its success clearly indicated the wisdom of using sunlight as a power source for space ventures.

Problems and solutions | Solar generation was the best way to power satellites and long distance space vehicles, but there were problems to overcome.

☐ Solar cells fail to generate power if they are allowed to become too hot. This is a severe problem in nearby space. Sunlight there is more than twice as bright as it is beneath the atmosphere on earth. By contrast, when the satellite is in the shadow of earth, the cells are exposed to extremely cold temperatures that can damage their circuitry.

☐ Because satellites and space vehicles travel at great speeds, every speck of dust they encounter has the impact of a bullet. Although space is relatively "clean," it's only a matter of time before such obstructions strike a space satellite.

☐ To produce power uniformly, solar generators require a great deal of flat surface area facing the sun. The generators also need protection from harm during the rigors of blast-off and the initial trip into space. These requirements are hard to meet on a small satellite.

☐ The solar generators of a satellite are not exposed to sunlight at all times—for example, when the satellite is in the shadow of earth. When they are not exposed to sunlight, they fail to generate power.

Patient research and expensive testing have provided ways to prepare solar cells for these strenuous service conditions. Every time a satellite circles the earth the solar generator will be subjected to extreme temperatures: over 100° Farenheit (38° Celsius) and more than 100° below zero (–73° Celsius). Such extremes of temperature, every ninety-odd minutes, would break up solar cell assemblies if they were not put together in special ways and mounted on very stable base material. Since overheating is the major problem, the cells are mounted upon a base material that will also conduct away excessive heat. In addition, each solar cell is often covered with a special glass plate that protects it from those wavelengths of light that would cause it to heat up.

Little can be done to prevent space particles from striking the solar panels. If the solar cells themselves are merely punctured or cracked, they will often continue to operate—if there is no short circuit. For space duty, the circuits are built to allow for damage to a few cells, without everything being put out of commission. This may result in less total power output, but it is better than wiring the system in such a way that damage to a few cells might break a circuit and ruin a space venture.

Solar cells have to be faced squarely toward the sun if they are to perform efficiently. This calls for large flat areas with motor controls enabling them to face the sun regardless of the satellite's position. But for reasons of economy and easy launching into space, satellite assemblies must also be as light and compact as possible.

When the power demands of a given satellite are not too great, there is often room on its outer surfaces to keep enough cells facing the sun. The satellite may be totally covered with cells. Those cells momentarily facing away from the sun simply do not generate power at that time. (They are all wired so that cells not generating power do not interfere with those cells that are.)

When power needs cannot be met merely by covering the outside of the satellite with cells, motorized solar panels have to be used. These panels constantly turn to face the sun. Once in space, the satellite often looks as if it has wings or paddles attached to it. But launching such an ungainly assembly would be most difficult. Therefore, during launching, the panels are folded or furled. After launching, special controls push away the outer packaging and the solar panels automatically unfold and face the sun. As there is almost no air where they operate, the

These satellite panels illustrate an interesting method of packaging and unfolding large surface areas in space. These are detection panels that record the presence of space dust.

extended panels will not be blown about in spite of the immense speed at which the satellite travels. Once in space, the panels keep themselves properly faced toward the sun, continuously generating power when the light falls on them. When the panels are in the earth's shadow, batteries, charged earlier by the solar panels, continue running the satellite system.

Since it costs over a thousand dollars to launch every pound of equipment that is orbited, the satellite must be as light as possible. Every material and device is thoroughly tested under simulated conditions on earth. Where very critical functions are involved, designers of satellite systems may install two complete sets of equipment in the craft. If one system breaks down (or needs to rest), the duplicate system will automatically take over. This is known as **redundancy** in space terminology. Pound for pound, many space satellites actually cost more than their weight in gold. But considering what they do, they are worth it.

SOLAR ENERGY AS A SCIENCE

If solar energy is to be used effectively, what it is and how much of it reaches us has to be measurable in some way—in exact, precise terms such as calories, or watts. (One of Albert Einstein's early contributions was to suggest that light was not a flowing wave, but consisted of specific units called photons.)

PUTTING NUMBERS ON IDEAS

Much early work in solar energy was done more by "feel" than by scientific method. But, fortunately, there were some good scientists at work in the early years. And they shared a tendency common to almost all scientists—to attach numbers to the things and events they study.

Solar insolation is the term used by scientists to identify sunlight that falls on a given place. A nineteenth-century American scientist named Samuel Langley established a way of measuring solar energy that was to be named after him. The **langley** offered a unit of measurement which scientists and engineers in various fields of study could convert into other numerical values as needed.

Where is sunlight the strongest? | It is common knowledge that sunlight is hotter over the Sahara than above the arctic circle.

Its strength varies from place to place—and weather conditions can deprive many places of its benefits with little warning.

Modern techniques of measurement, and past records of weather conditions around the world, are combined to provide reliable data about the output of solar energy almost anywhere in the world.

The sun is strongest in the United States during the summer, and in most parts of the country its yield, on any sunny day, ranges from 500 to 700 langleys. In the shorter days and poor weather of December, this average drops to between 100 and 300 langleys.

Weather conditions must be taken into account to predict the potential usefulness of solar radiation in any particular place. Weather data collected over the years provides the information needed to determine the solar insolation that can be reliably counted upon in any one location.

How reliable is solar energy? | Even though sunlight can now be reliably measured, the effects of location and weather make it variable. It still does not offer constant power at the throw of a switch. And most scientists who deal with power are more at home dealing with the many energy sources that do offer this convenience.

Though there is now much greater interest in harnessing the sun's energy, it is still considered an unreliable power supply (even if it is free). Those impressive numbers about the raw value of sunlight are all very well, but there's been much grumbling over the question of how to get all that energy out of it in usable form.

How efficient is solar energy? | Some of the engineers and scientists doing this grumbling are used to working with machines and engines that have been refined over the years to yield back a good return of the energy it takes to run them. They have a high **efficiency of conversion.** Hydroelectric generators running on the free force of downhill-running water are among the systems that offer high returns.

In the mid-1950s, the Bell Laboratories produced the first

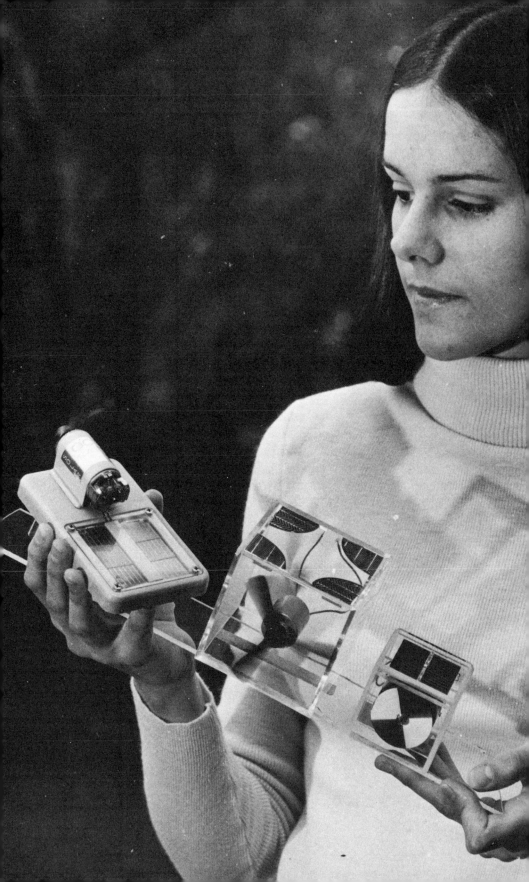

solar cells that would convert 5 percent of the light-energy falling on them into useful electricity. Engineers who were getting much higher returns from other sources were quite understandably not impressed. But the real magnitude of the accomplishment escaped them. These first cells were over five times more efficient in the conversion of sunlight than the natural process, **photosynthesis.** In reality, for a first effort, it was an excellent beginning. And within only a decade, the efficiency of solar cells would more than double—and would continue rising!

The natural environment, by contrast, has a solar conversion efficiency usually well below 1 percent. Perhaps the most efficient of plants are certain forms of kelp (sea plants) and the water hyacinth, and their ability to tap solar radiation for their notably rapid growth hovers around only 1 percent. Such crops as corn convert only a fraction of this, and most cereals even less. Yet even with such "low" efficiency, solar energy is responsible for the survival and development of the human race as well as all other life on earth. So we should look upon the 5-percent solar cell in its proper light—as an accomplishment over five times better than "nature's way."

The grumbling will diminish. Some of the old ways are simply going to become history, because of the growing scarcity and high costs of fuels—and the damage some of them inflict upon our world. And technology will give us better ways to utilize solar energy, and make it increasingly attractive.

**Three commercial solar demonstrators
whose solar cells are strong enough
to power their motors on a hazy day.
(Items are included in Materials List.)**

SOLAR ENERGY ON EARTH

The exploration of space finally brought widespread attention to the advantages solar energy had to offer. Now, other events have brought even more attention to the important role solar energy can play in our lives.

The energy crisis | By the mid-1960s, it had become common knowledge that we would stifle ourselves if we continued to burn our fuels in wasteful ways. At the same time, we awakened to long-ignored warnings about how fast we were depleting these fuels. And fuels were all the more important because they were now being used to make fertilizer and new materials like plastics.

At first, pollution affected us the most. It became the stuff of real-life horror stories. Hundreds of people died when windless stagnant skies blanketed cities with smog from the overuse of fuels. Sealed-up buildings became unlivably hot as their air-conditioning systems failed during the drops in power called "brownouts."

"Quick-fix" suggestions were plentiful. Vast coal resources existed, a hundred years' worth—if we were willing to dig deeper,

This solar-charged flashlight is included in the Materials List.

**Solar One house at Newark, Delaware.
The small shed to the right of the house
contains batteries for energy storage.**

or wreck surface land by strip-mining. Nuclear reactors—the only power source not linked directly to solar energy—were already being built. Many people felt that nuclear energy would be a genuine solution to our growing needs for more energy and a cleaner environment. Nuclear power would be clean, reliable, and relatively long-lasting. But, by the mid-1970s, experience with nuclear power plants suggested problems that had not earlier been foreseen. Their supposed economic benefits were not being realized. There was the problem of how to dispose of nuclear wastes (which can remain dangerous for generations). How could we insure that nuclear wastes or by-products would not be used by destructive people to threaten society? Though many scientists and engineers could be found to praise the potential benefits of nuclear technology, a growing number of equally competent scientists admitted they were "scared to death of it!"

And, lastly, the belief in nuclear power as being "unlimited" wasn't accurate. Some of the raw resources of nuclear power were equally subject to exhaustion, or extremely difficult to deal with. It began to appear that even nuclear energy would be but another superficial answer, and a dangerous one at that. But falling back on depletable resources—coal and oil—was not a good solution, either. A demonstration of that fact came even sooner than we expected.

In the early 1970s, the politics practiced among nations took a new turn. An embargo on oil imports to the United States gave most Americans a lesson in what life might be like without enough oil to fuel now routine daily energy needs, or to supply the raw material for fertilizer and plastics. Long lines of cars at filling stations snarled traffic everywhere and soured the tempers of the most patient people, for the United States is a nation on wheels. It was clear that the solution could no longer be left to future generations. And the solution must be long-lasting. A great many more people began to look seriously at what the sun had to offer.

One early fruit of this attention was the beginning of new and better-funded research intended to hasten the time when solar energy could be put to use in a practical way and in significant amounts. Among early efforts was an attempt to organize what was already known about solar energy and to increase the understanding of it in areas that have been neglected.

TECHNIQUES FOR USING SOLAR ENERGY

Two basic approaches | The technology of solar energy has been organized into two basic approaches called **direct conversion,** and **indirect conversion.**

Direct conversion takes place when energy is derived from sunlight itself and is used immediately. Solar cells, for example, convert sunlight directly into electrical power. And sunlight can be converted directly into heat for climate control in office buildings and homes.

Indirect conversion involves tapping energy from such sources as the wind, falling water, ocean currents, and temperature differences between surface and deep water. All of these sources are natural forms of energy that were initially brought about by solar radiation.

Hydroelectric power is the best-known example of indirect conversion. The water wheel that once powered the miller's grindstones was using indirect energy from the sun. (The flowing water used by the wheel was originally evaporated from the seas by the power of the sun.)

USING SUNLIGHT TO HEAT HOMES

The heating of dwellings by direct conversion has long been an ideal application of solar energy—particularly because more fuel is used to heat our homes than is used to run our various forms of transportation. But there is one problem. The need to heat a dwelling is greatest in the colder climates where the sun's rays are less effective. In warmer climates, of course, the situation is just the reverse. The need is often to shield the dwelling from the sun's heat, and to lower the inside temperature.

In recent years, however, methods have been worked out so that dwellings can be both heated and cooled by the energy

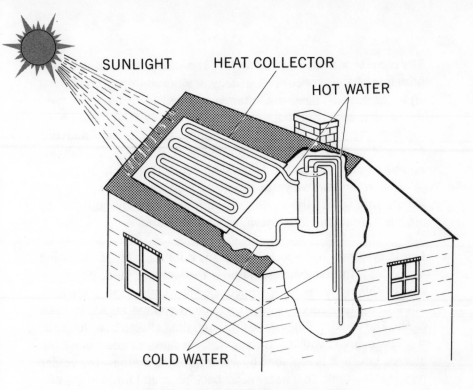

SUNLIGHT   HEAT COLLECTOR

HOT WATER

COLD WATER

A typical solar-heated hot-water system.

of sunlight almost anywhere. The sun's heat falls on heat-absorbing collectors. It is then converted into a form that can be moved and sent to different areas—or be stored for use during the night or during periods of bad weather. There is now also a way to convert the energy in the stored heat into forms that can cool the dwelling during hot weather.

Now that we can measure solar radiation, we can accurately calculate and design solar climate-control systems in our buildings.

At this time, a wide variety of solar heat collectors are being developed and marketed. But regardless of how they work, most have one thing in common: they are located on a sun-exposed roof, where they convert solar radiation into **convected heat.** This can be pumped from the collector to a place where it will be used or stored.

Structure of a solar heat collector | The collector is built on the principle of a greenhouse. It usually is a boxed-in tray containing pipes or tubes. These are often blackened in order to convert the radiant energy of the sun into convected heat. A clear covering over the collector admits the sun's radiant energy and discourages its reradiation to the outside—and it prevents outside air movement from sweeping away the collected heat.

There are two ways to move the heat absorbed by the collectors throughout the system. It can be moved by liquid or by air. Both are technically known as **working fluids.**

Liquid systems | If the working fluid is a liquid, a lot of plumbing is involved. In many cases, water is the working fluid. When the sun is shining, water is pumped slowly through the system. It flows from the collectors to an insulated storage tank and back again. The working fluid passes through the collectors, which heat it a few degrees with each pass. It then flows to the top of the storage tank and is replaced by water from the bottom—the colder region of the tank. This water flows back up to and through the collectors where it is in turn heated a bit more and returned to the top of the storage tank. In time, on a good sunny day, the water in the tank can rise to as much as 180° Fahrenheit (82° Celsius). And even on a hazy or dull day, the water in the tank usually gets hot enough to handle normal day and night heating needs.

One way to improve storage is to house the hot-water tank in a well-insulated box that is large enough to contain as well a considerable pile of small stones, or other heat-absorbing material. The tank accumulates the heat from the solar collectors, and transfers much of it into the pile of stones. Since the box is insulated, the heat of the rock pile is trapped, and the temperature of the whole assembly gradually rises.

A conventional hot-air heating system in the house can then use the heat from the rock. Air is circulated through the heated rocks and then throughout the living areas of the building. A standard gas or oil heating system is usually installed in addition, particularly in colder northern climates. This serves as a back-up source of heat during long periods of dark winter weather when the solar heating system cannot generate all that is needed.

Modern solar cells and panels.
The big round cell in the middle is 4 in. (10 cm) in diameter.
(Several items appear in Materials List.)

In extremely cold areas, the liquid that flows through the collectors—which are exposed to the cold—may be an antifreeze solution. In this case, a separate system known as a **heat exchanger** uses the antifreeze (such as alcohol or glycol) instead of water. The heat exchanger itself is usually a many-looped coil of copper tubing built into the bottom of the storage tank. Its input and output fittings extend to the outside of the water-storage tank. The rooftop collector's water lines are connected to the heat-exchanger connections, and antifreeze solution is put in these lines. This fluid—moved with a separate pump—is circulated through the collectors and the heat exchanger. Heat brought from the collectors is conducted through the copper walls of the heat-exchanger tubing into the cold water in the bottom of the tank, which then rises, by **thermal convection,** to the top of the storage tank.

All-air systems | The solar collectors for a hot-air system transfer heat with air instead of liquid. They are designed to heat air that is blown through the collectors. Air is thus considered the "working fluid" of the system.

In this system, a large bin of rock or other material is used instead of a water tank to store the collected heat—although a water tank can be included for conversion of the heat in the rocks to hot water. The air that was warmed in the collector is blown through the rock pile, where the heat is transferred to the cooler rocks. Then the cooled air is returned for another pass through the collectors for reheating.

Both liquid and air systems have their advantages and disadvantages. The liquid system involves considerable and often complicated plumbing that may leak. If there is danger of freezing, a heat exchanger must be added. But the use of liquid to move and store heat still tends to be the more efficient. Both approaches to the solar heating of dwellings are widely used today.

Some engineers are trying to find new ways that use less energy to move and handle working fluids. Having noted that heated air and water rise, they reason that a system designed to take advantage of this behavior will reduce the need to pump liquids and air. For example, if large window areas are located on the south side of buildings, they will admit the maximum heat. Tanks of water, skillfully hidden in and near the walls, will absorb this heat, and give it back during cooler periods. Another way to use less energy is to set hot-water tanks and storage chambers higher than conventional solar collectors, allowing them to take advantage of the tendency of hot water to rise. This process is known as **thermal syphoning.** Water heated in the collectors will rise in the plumbing and find its way into the top of the higher storage tank. At the same time, the cooler water in the bottom of the tank "falls" through the plumbing into the bottom of the collector for reheating—then it will repeat the cycle and rise in the system to the storage tank.

The approaches to solar heating just described are known as "passive" techniques—as opposed to "active" techniques. The active techniques are the heat-and-pump systems which ignore, or do not seek to utilize, the energy-saving advantages of thermal syphoning or window-created heat. Passive approaches are still quite new in the field of solar heating. However, they are promising, and potentially simpler in design than the active techniques.

Solar cooling | Solar collectors can also be used to remove heat from buildings during hot weather by simply running the whole system "in reverse." The working fluid is circulated back through the solar collectors during the cooler nighttime hours. Heat from the working fluid is then exhausted outdoors. During hot days, the working fluid in the solar collectors is not circulated, so outside heat is not brought indoors. (In systems using liquid instead of air as a working fluid, some kind of shield or protection may be called for since the collectors can become too hot if the heat they collect is not removed.) At night, when outside temperatures are cooler, the collector system is turned on in order to send the warmed water from the storage tank through the now cool panels on the roof—where the heat is discharged to the outdoors. By the return of the hot daytime weather (when the circulation system is stopped), the storage tank—and its pile of rock—has cooled off and is ready to begin collecting and removing heat from the dwelling's inside air by circulating it through the cooled rock.

In all-air solar heating systems, cool nighttime air can be pumped through the storage pile with the same result. This process is limited to climates where the need for cooling is not excessive. (Other techniques exist for removing heat in warmer climates. But they are much more complex and costly. They involve special kinds of refrigeration technology that must be incorporated into the solar heating system.)

Insulation | At the heart of the effective solar energy system for both the heating and cooling of buildings is good insulation. Good insulation will keep the solar-heated home comfortable for long

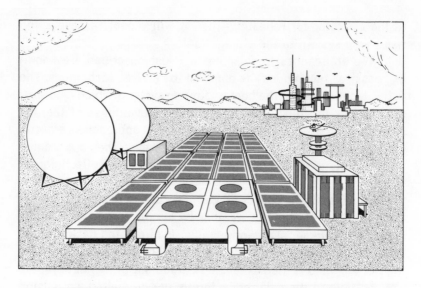

In the future, whole communities may be powered from centrally-located solar power plants.

periods of time during dank winter days. Good insulation in the walls, ceilings, and near the foundations prevents heat from passing through the walls and roof of a building. Thus, less energy is needed to warm it in the winter and cool it in the summer. Engineers interested in the passive approach take every measure to insulate the foundation on the outside, so that heat trapped indoors does not escape into the earth during very cold winters in northern areas.

Economics | It would be nice to depend totally on free solar energy, and thus be independent of the utility companies (and their charges). But—in all but the most balmy climates—the most that can be realized is a 75 to 85 percent reduction in consumption of conventional fuels. There will be times during any winter when the sun shines only briefly in a day—or not at all for several weeks. Collectors and supporting systems able to handle all your heating needs throughout such periods of "solar drought" are simply not yet practical or affordable. You could dig a large hole under or near your home to house a huge rock pile and tank. But it would have to be as big as a swimming pool—and the cost would be staggering.

Solar heating and cooling systems presently cost more to buy and install than conventional fuel-powered systems. To be economically practical, savings on fuel costs must be greater in the long run than the expense of installing a solar energy system.

And, in the long run, you might make more money in interest on a savings account than you would save by heating with solar energy. But even if economics may control the degree to which solar energy is used, lower-cost practical systems will continually be developed. And with the increasing cost of conventional fuels— and their growing scarcity--the use of solar energy for climate control will be further stimulated. There is little doubt that, in time, entire communities will be serviced by centrally located solar-powered systems serving the needs of many dwellings and buildings.

Early experiments in solar heating | An experimental solar-heated house, built in Cambridge, Massachusetts, by the Massachusetts Institute of Technology, used water as a storage medium, and found that it was sufficient to handle about 90 percent of the building's winter heating needs. During bad weather, however, an electric hot-water heater had to be used to keep the system warm enough to heat the house.

Another experimental house heated by solar energy was built at Princeton, New Jersey, by Dr. Maria Telkes. It employed a low-melting-point salt as a heat-storage material. This material, known as Glauber's salts, is able to store more heat for its volume than can water. In the Telkes house, air heated by the solar collector was blown through a chamber in which containers of Glauber's salts absorbed heat from the air. During periods when the sun was not shining, cool air from the dwelling was circulated through the same storage bins to collect heat from the Glauber's salts and convey it back into the living areas of the house.

Perhaps the first commercially practical solar-heated homes were built in the Washington, D.C., area by Dr. Harry Thomason. In these, water is used to convey heat from the solar collector on the outside of the house to a big storage tank located in a large underground chamber filled with small rocks. Dr. Thomason has done much to further this field by reducing his concepts to levels of practical application and reliability. In recent years, he has refined his design, and he has published numerous plans and information about related technology to aid builders wishing to use solar climate control.

FURTHER USES OF SOLAR ENERGY

POWER FROM THE WIND

Wind power is an example of indirect conversion of solar energy. If you talk about wind power in the prairies or plains of the western United States, you won't awaken much excitement. It's not a new idea to people there. In Holland, you can often see—and hear—the creaking, slow-moving blades of windmills which have been pumping water for centuries. These people take wind power for granted. But many of them may not realize that wind power comes from solar energy. Solar heat, rising from the earth, creates thermal air currents which help to create wind. This form of solar energy is one we've used throughout time. It propelled Columbus's ships to America and Magellan around the world. And windmills pumped water on the early prairie farms. Even today, several manufacturers produce water-pumping windmills, and at least one American manufacturer of wind generators exists. With renewed interest in energy conservation, several foreign manufacturers are producing wind generators. Many of these generators are quite large and can produce enough energy to handle the needs of several households—if good winds can be relied upon.

The wind doesn't blow all the time or everywhere, and its average rate varies with location. And unlike sunlight—whose maximum output is a fixed figure on a bright sunny day—wind

power varies, from the force of a light zephyr, to that of a property-damaging hurricane. Sunlight isn't likely to damage well-made solar panels or heat collectors, but a hundred-mile-an-hour wind can rip a poorly mounted windmill right out of the ground and run off with it.

But even with these problems, the winds can be usefully employed—and tamed—with the right equipment. Serious research is now under way to make windmills, and their generators, better. And many home-engineers are trying new ways to harness the wind. Kits for converting old water-pumping mills to electricity-producing machines are now appearing in the ads of "do-it-yourself" mechanics magazines. Their users are not too concerned about how efficiently these mills convert wind to energy—just so long as they put out enough juice. (After all, this source of power is free.)

The National Aeronautics and Space Administration (NASA) has erected an impressive wind generator in Ohio with an output of 100 kilowatts. NASA scientists are also experimenting with other designs, such as S-shaped rotors that (standing upright) spin in the wind no matter what direction it is coming from. NASA recently made a new kind of rotor that looks like an upside-down egg beater. Its advantage is that wind hitting it from any direction will turn it and run a generator mounted in its base. Older fan- and blade-type mills must be facing the wind to operate, and so special tail assemblies are needed to shift the blades so that they always aim into the wind. This also calls for rather fancy devices to carry the current from a generator that is never sitting in one direction for very long. Their new "egg beater" mill, which solves these problems, is also much more attractive looking. This should please those who have expressed concern about the visual impact of big, mechanically unsightly windmills on an otherwise natural environment.

This "egg-beater" is an experimental vertical axis windmill for converting wind power to electricity. The blades rotate in almost any wind to provide energy for a typical single-family house.

The future of wind power will become more promising as new techniques and better ways to store wind energy are developed. Storage is important for we still want power on demand—at the throw of a switch.

Some modern-day technology does lend itself to wind generation, even when output varies. One example is the recharging of batteries for any devices that have long periods of rest. An electric vehicle that is used only during the day can have its batteries recharged overnight. As long as an average overnight output of energy can be relied upon, the vehicle's batteries will receive enough energy, if only in spurts, as the wind speeds change. By the end of the night, enough energy is stored to do the next day's chores.

Even though the problems of variable output still have to be solved, many scientists feel that wind energy could one day generate twice the current output of all our hydroelectric power facilities.

WATER POWER

Hydroelectric power has already almost reached its limit in this country. To extract much more energy would require building more dams and the flooding of land for reservoirs. Many people feel the environment can't take much more of this without reducing the quality of life. Attractive and ecologically important rural and wilderness areas have become scarce. It may be that trading them for more water power isn't worth the trade.

But in some cases a waterwheel may still be the answer. For instance, a waterwheel may supply enough power to handle local chores. Many old historic miller's waterwheels have been converted to electrical generation. "Electrified," such an old mill can often take care of all a farmer's needs—and perhaps those of several nearby farms!

**NASA 100 kw
experimental wind generator,
at Sanduski, Ohio.**

And dropping a small drumlike wheel into a running stream can provide enough power for a small generator to light the lights in a cabin, run a small refrigerator, or provide power for operating television and radio receivers. Riggings and beams at shoreside can support the "mini-millwheel" without damage to the nearby environment. The wheel is quieter than a noisy gasoline generator and does away with the added chore of hauling in fuel—and its output is constant!

ENERGY FROM THE SEA

The sun transfers energy to the sea in several ways. Among these is the creation of currents due largely to wind activity and temperature differences at various levels in ocean water. Scientists are looking into possible ways these forms of energy could be harnessed and used.

At certain locations, the surface water (heated by the sun) is much warmer than water many fathoms deeper. It may be possible to use this heat to operate large floating electrical-generation plants permanently anchored in such places offshore. Transmission cables, lying on the bottom of the ocean, would transfer the energy produced to the mainland where it would be fed into the power system. Heat-exchange systems, which would derive energy from the temperature differences between surface (warm) and deep (cold) water, are being studied. This approach might offer efficient returns for the effort, and the power supplied would be reasonably constant.

Harnessing the tides is another idea that has intrigued people for years. (The French have operated large tidal electric-power-generating systems.) Equally intriguing is the effort to get useful energy from continuous ocean currents. Because such currents are usually quite slow, much more study will be needed before we can answer the question of just how practical this would be.

SOLAR DESALTING OF SEAWATER

This process produces not energy but a product—fresh water. It is not a new idea. The desalting plant in Chile described earlier worked for many years. Experiments being carried out today involve largely the same techniques, using newer materials. The Australian government has conducted work in this area for a number of years. Systems for desalting water are unfortunately quite "land hungry." They call for vast areas of open land for the installation of ponds and facilities for evaporation and condensation of water. In many areas where desalting would be an excellent solution to the problem of scarce fresh water, land is too precious to spare. Work is being done to find new techniques that will reduce the need for so much land area.

PHOTOVOLTAIC GENERATION: NEW DIRECTIONS

The use of solar cells did the most to attract broad attention to the potential value of solar energy. But there's more to be told about the direct conversion of light to electricity.

The silicon cell still remains attractive for its good conversion efficiency. But making cells cut from over-grown ingots means that the finished cells are limited in size—to the largest slice that can be cut from the silicon ingot. The ingots are grown bigger now, but the largest single cell is only four inches in diameter. And although costs have dropped, these cells will never be as inexpensive as other promising techniques now being developed.

In one new approach, the thin material that makes up the base of the completed solar cell is drawn out of the silicon "melt" as a continuous ribbon. If this material could be drawn very thin, the cell would actually be less fragile. (Spun glass is an example of a rigid material made flexible by making it extremely fine.) The thickness of the base is not important to the function of the solar cell, so the thinner it can be made, the less of the expensive raw material is required per cell.

And, by being able to "pull" cells in ribbons as long as desired, one long solar cell can often provide all the current necessary for any particular job. This will reduce the need for expensive intricate wiring and soldering of a solar panel. These cells would also be more reliable and rugged, for there would be fewer junctions that could be broken.

"Printed-circuit" solar cells | Printed circuits are so called because there are no wires to break loose; the electricity is conducted through strips that are printed or etched into place on a sheet of non-conducting material. In effect, solder is printed on base boards to serve all interconnecting circuit needs.

Printed-circuit cadmium sulphide "thin-film" cells were an early discovery. They are not yet as efficient as silicon cells, but they have several advantages over silicon cells:

☐ They can be made in almost any size desired.

☐ They are much less fragile than silicon cells; they cannot "break" the way glasslike silicon cells can. Even if something punches a hole through one of the cells, unless a main junction is broken at the same time (or there is a short circuit), the cell may very well continue operating with little loss of power.

☐ Printed-circuitry techniques can be used both to mass-produce individual cells and to produce complete solar panels of given outputs. The base material is a piece of thin plastic film, and all the interconnecting hookups can be a basic part of the printed circuit.

However, thin-film cells do present a problem even though they offer lower costs, simplicity of design, and reliability. Because of their lower efficiency, they take up a larger area than silicon cells to do a given job. On earth, this is not as big a problem as it is in space. But it is the reason that mass-power schemes using this kind of photovoltaic generator have been slow in developing. Thin-film cadmium generators are still much less than 10 percent efficient. The area for solar exposure needed —even for silicon cells with a 16 percent efficiency of conversion—would be enormous compared to the space a conventional power plant requires.

A solar panel uses sunlight to power this handie-talkie.

Electric power from orbit | One "far out" idea for generating mass power with solar energy is now being studied. It involves the making of an enormous array of solar panels—several miles in each direction. This construction would be launched into space in pieces (using the "space shuttle" craft). Finally, it would be assembled at its orbit-location. This vast photovoltaic collector would be aimed at the sun at all times by using appropriate machinery. Several such stations could be placed in orbit at various positions around the globe so that the sun would always be shining on some while others were in the shadow of the earth. The energy collected would be converted to microwave power, then beamed back to earth-based receiving stations. At earth level, the power would be reconverted to useful electrical energy that could be fed into the conventional power system.

The idea of getting electricity directly from the sun—particularly from solar cells—has always stirred the imagination. Because no moving parts are involved, solar cells could in theory do this remarkable thing forever, and do it free!

But only now do scientists and engineers realize that getting energy from the sun is practical. And the fact that our other sources of energy are in decline has turned their imagination loose.

Squirrel power runs a radio. Squirrel energy comes from solar energy— through the food chain.

SCIENTIFIC DREAMS

This section outlines a few scientific dreams, to give some idea of just how far scientists think we can go.

SOLAR "FARMING"

One proposal for producing massive amounts of electrical energy from the sun takes us right back to the land—arid land that is not useful for much else—the Southwest desert of the United States.

Some scientists envision a vast "farm" consisting of row upon row of solar collectors. These would use **parabolic reflectors** to collect solar heat and concentrate it to the point where high temperatures were generated in a working fluid pumped through the collectors. The heated fluid would flow through conventional large-scale engine-generator systems. These systems would use the heat to produce electric power that could be sent wherever it was needed.

It is possible that small amounts of the energy produced could be diverted to provide power for irrigation pumps. Deep ground water brought to the surface could be used to "regreen" the arid land nearby, making real farmland in and near the solar farm. (Cattle could initially find shade beneath the raised solar collectors!)

Such a solar farm would produce prodigious amounts of power—and without damaging the environment.

A similar approach that has been suggested is the use of vast rows of ground-based mirrors—all motor-controlled and timed so that they move with the sun during the day. Each mirror would beam its reflected sunlight precisely to a collecting device on a nearby tower. The intense heat formed by the light of all these computer-controlled mirrors beamed to a single spot on the tower would be used to drive turbines or other forms of engine-generators. If many of these farms were scattered over the desert, clouds over one farm would not seriously alter the general output, so long as other farms in the system were under clear skies.

ENERGY FROM PHOTOSYNTHESIS

Photosynthesis is nature's way of using solar radiation. In the past, we have tended to ignore just how vast and important a process this is. (And we are aware that the process is less efficient than other means of producing energy.) Most scientists pay little attention to the role photosynthesis could play in meeting today's pressing energy needs. Perhaps this is because they tend to rely on machines, devices, and circuitry hardware to create power. But some biologists are proposing new directions that seem promising.

Biochemical sources of electricity | Many a biologist has proposed looking to biological sources of energy, and has had to deal with skeptics who doubt that electricity can really be procured from living things. And most biologists do feel that other energy products are worth considering first. But—yes—there may well be ways to derive electricity from biological processes. (The electric eel can deliver a good jolt of electricity!)

As early as 1961, scientists were aware that certain decomposing organic matter produces measurable amounts of electricity. Several forms of biochemical fuel cells have been constructed that can operate such things as radio receivers by using current released in the breakdown of the components of sewage. The output is small, but greater than the output of the selenium cells in early light meters which led to the development of the silicon cell. Little in this area has been done as yet, but it will no longer be ignored.

Replenishable fuels from sunlight | Another area for attention is that of the creation of useful and even new fuels from the products of photosynthesis. We have become so dependent on our fuel-burning engines that we would find it very difficult to give them up. But our fossil fuels will finally give out! If we are to continue using such engines, it's obvious that we need a new process to meet their energy needs.

Many sun-grown organic materials and by-products—wood, plant fibers, paper, and even sewage—could be processed to yield liquid and gaseous fuels. The garbage and trash we now pay to have carted away could become a valuable resource for the manufacture of fuels for our engines. And, unlike fossil fuels, these new fuels could be clean-burning—a partial solution to the problem of air pollution.

Using "nature's way" | In the mid-1970s, NASA tried using water hyacinth to process the outflow of a sewage treatment plant and turn it into clean water.

In the United States, water hyacinth has long been considered a frightful foreign weed. It was loosed into our Southern waterways in the late nineteenth century and became a positive menace. Because it is such an efficient user of sunlight, it grows very fast. It chokes the waterways and millions of dollars are spent each year to remove it. Laws have even been passed to forbid its transportation over state lines!

Solar operated "lazy Susan" turntable (called a climostat) rotates to give all sides of the plant equal light. In the background a solar operated pump aerates an aquarium.

Even before the NASA experiment, some scientists believed the water hyacinth plants might yield valuable fuels, cattle feeds, and fertilizers. But until NASA scientists did something practical with the weed, no one took seriously the useful potential of the plant that is so efficient in using sunlight.

"Nature's way" can sometimes be sped up. Even in the hyacinth, photosynthesis is admittedly a slow process. Maximum production of plants is usually well below 1 percent. But scientists around the world have been tampering with the process in such ways as increasing the supply of carbon dioxide for test plants. And they have been examining the possibilities for obtaining food and other useful products from such highly efficient plants as algae and seaweed. Early results suggest that it is possible to increase the growth rates of some plants to many times over their normal yield.

Photosynthesis converts more solar energy than any other process on earth; perhaps one of the most beneficial long range uses of solar energy will be to go back to "nature's way" as a starting point, and give mother nature a helping hand.

SOLAR ENERGY PROJECTS

Just how important a role solar energy will play in our lives depends on how soon and how well we use it. This is the important stage—finding out which are the best ways to use this technology. But it will take trial and error and experimenting with existing systems to discover which new materials and techniques are really going to work.

Reading is important—to profit from the work others have done. But an equally important part of learning about solar energy is experimentation.

SCHOOL PROJECTS

Some solar energy projects—while they can be excellent home-projects—may require materials you are less likely to find around the house or at local stores. These projects may also be more costly. Such projects include running motors on solar energy, making models that involve motors and solar cells, and building high-temperature solar furnace models. However, these experiments are ideal school projects which can be shared by many students.

BUILDING A SOLAR FURNACE

When you ignite a piece of paper or char some wood by means of a magnifying glass, the heat is obtained by concentrating an

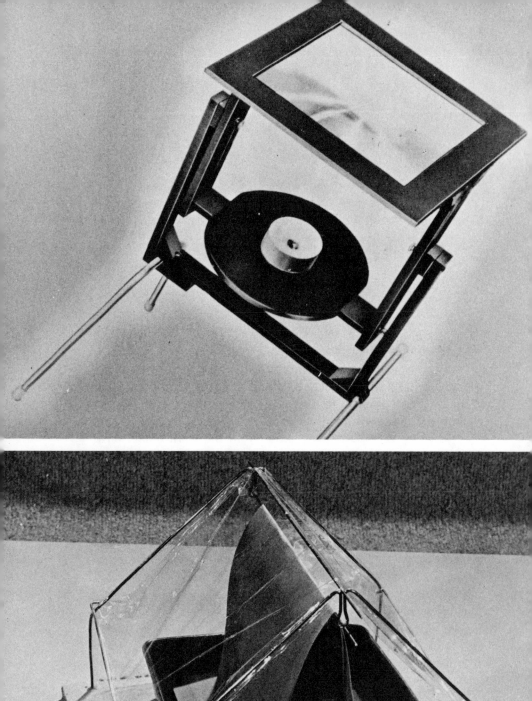

area of sunlight onto a much smaller spot. The larger the area that is concentrated onto a small spot, the greater the amount of heat you can obtain. The Materials List gives a source for a large Fresnel lens (pronounced FRAY-NEL, after the French physicist Augustin Jean Fresnel). The List also gives a source for building plans for a very simple but effective high-temperature solar furnace. With this furnace, and lots of sunlight, you can conduct experiments that include the melting of metals. Although this furnace is but a miniature edition of a large solar furnace located in the French Pyrenees, it is able to generate very high temperatures. Only a large forge or an oxyacetylene torch is able to generate heat at such temperatures using conventional fuels.

MAKING A SOLAR STILL

Making a model solar still is relatively simple. It can be made of several coat hangers, some plastic wrap, a blackened aluminum pan, a piece of dark terry-cloth towel, and two shallow saucers or film cans. The still is placed in the sun with salt water in the blackened pan. As the water is sucked up by the terry-cloth towel, fresh water will evaporate due to the sun's heat. It will condense on the sides of the plastic-wrap "tent," and then drip off into the catch-saucers located near the drip-off points. The same experiment can be made using a scoop of damp soil or mud (instead of the terry-cloth). Water will evaporate from the sun-heated soil, and condense on the tent's walls.

Above: solar furnace using Fresnel lens.
Below: solar still is a tent made of
plastic wrap and coat-hanger wire.
Wire is bent to form the two end
frames and to hold the top layer taut.
Note blotting paper in tray for speed-
ing up evaporation of salt water.
Moisture will condense on plastic
wrap and drip down sides of tent.

SOLAR GENERATORS AND MOTORS

Being able to run a small motor on sunlight is perhaps the most stimulating experiment of them all. Watching a small motor whir away in the palm of your hand—powered by several solar cells exposed to sunlight or a tungsten lamp—raises thoughts of boats and automobiles, perhaps even airships of the future, operating for extended periods on this free energy source. While the realizations of such visions are still in the future, it is not difficult to build working models of boats and vehicles, and other motor-powered devices that can run on sunlight.

Such models call for the use of suitable miniature DC (direct current) motors capable of handling a given task, and enough solar cells to provide the electrical current needed to power the motors. Two kinds of motors will be discussed here. One is a motor whose shaft is able to turn propellers and do light work at high speed. The other is a "gear-head" motor, in which the output speed of the motor is geared down so it can do harder work by turning at slower speeds.

When not called upon to exert any real **torque,** either of these motors will operate on as little as one solar cell. To test the motor so that you may see the motor shaft turn, attach the propeller from a model plane to the motor's shaft and hook the wires from a solar cell to the motor terminals. Then simply hold it out in the sun.

Running a model boat on sunlight is easily done. Simply hook a small motor directly onto the propeller shaft of the model. Many commercial boat models sold in toy and hobby stores come equipped with motor drives. The motors that come with the kits usually will not work on solar cells, but these can be easily replaced by similar ones given in the Materials List.

Above: small motor with solar shingle runs a gearbox by a magnetic coupling. Below: the same device powers a "lazy Susan" turntable with plug-in module (no shingled cells). See page 75 for a lazy Susan "climostat."

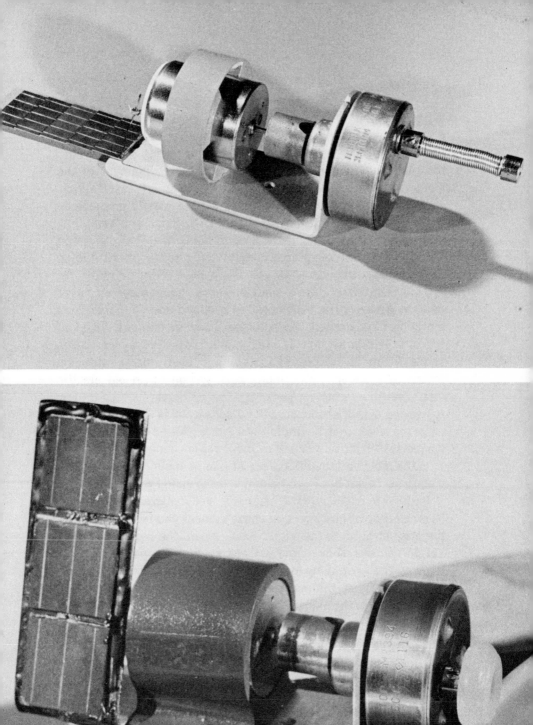

Take care to align the solar-drive motor well so that there is no binding or side-friction that would prevent it from running. A good way to connect the motor shaft to the propeller shaft in the boat is to use a short length of flexible spring jammed onto the motor shaft and the propeller shaft. The alignment of the motor and propeller shafts will thus not be so critical. If small, shaft-sized springs are hard to find, flexible plastic or medical-grade latex tubing will do reasonably well. Small shaft-coupling springs and plastic tubing are sold in many model airplane and hobby shops—and electronic supply stores sell a plastic tubing called "spaghetti."

In cases where more shaft power is required to run larger models, power rather than speed is required and so a gear-head motor will be needed. Several gear-head motors are listed at the end of this section. If their higher costs prove a problem, you can use a simple straight-output shaft motor with the inexpensive encapsulated motor-gear system of an old electric clock (see illustration on page 58). This will create a high-torque, low-speed output shaft that will do considerable work.

The hookup of the motor and clock gear-head drive is both simple and effective. A small cylindrical alnico magnet is jammed onto the motor shaft with a piece of plastic tubing that will make a snug fit. Test it out (run the motor up to speed with a solar cell or battery) to make sure the magnet is well centered on the shaft. (A small drop of quick-setting epoxy cement can be used to keep the magnet tight on the shaft.) Next, mount the motor and magnet behind the clock-motor gearbox so that the magnet almost touches the protruding dome of the gearbox. When the motor spins the magnet, the magnet's field turns the gears in the clock gearbox, which then slowly turns the output shaft. This shaft can then be hooked up to whatever small device you wish to power. The output of the gearbox may be a tiny shaft or a small gear. If it already has a gear that will not come off easily, use an oversize coupling right over the gear. At a hobby shop you can select as snug-fitting a coupling as possible—or gears that will mesh with the gear already on the shaft!

With the motors listed at the back of this section you will be in a position to put together many models that will operate on solar cells powered by sunlight. Following are some examples of solar-powered operating models that will give you ideas for making your own devices.

SOLAR-OPERATED SUN TRACKING SYSTEM

This device keeps itself in constant alignment with the sun. A 5 to 20 rpm (revolutions per minute) portescap (shown in illustration) or Namiki gear-head motor is the best choice for making the most refined version of this device, but they are more costly than others. The lower-cost Hankscraft gear-head motors will work, but will work best using a tracking solar panel made with larger 2-centimeter square cells rather than the 1-by-2-centimeter cells shown in the illustration on page 62. The four-cell hookup illustrated is used both to power and guide the device. A light-baffle between the divided banks of cells (two to each side) causes light to fall on one side or the other (both sides together, when the alignment is achieved). This causes the voltage to the motor to change its **polarity,** depending upon the sun's relative position to the divided solar bank. It is this changing of polarity that causes the motor to "hunt" for a proper alignment position. Thus, solar energy is used not only to run the system, but also to provide the automatic guidance that forces the system to stay in solar alignment.

SELF-TRACKING SOLAR ENGINE, FURNACE, OR GENERATOR

This tracking system can be used with solar energy models when it is necessary to keep them aimed at the sun. The solar driven Stirling-cycle engine illustrated on page 70 is kept in alignment using this system of guidance. The four-cell "tracker" is attached to the rim of the solar collector bowl, with its lead wires carrying its "signal" down to the gear-head motor that drives the gearing which moves the whole array.

This device can be used to "track" the solar furnace described earlier. A low-speed (about ½ to 1 rpm) gear-head motor can be lashed to its gimbal so that the tracking-unit solar panel

LUGS TO MOTOR TERMINAL

Left: a portescap motor bearing the
cell assembly shown in the diagram.
At its right is a hankscraft gear-head motor
with a tracking panel using shingled
cells on each side of a baffle for
higher voltage and larger output.
Above: self-tracking solar generator can
generate enough power to keep the model
train running all day. Concentrated
light increases output of solar panel.

will power the motor and keep the furnace's Fresnel lens in constant focus at the right place, within the target area of the furnace throughout the day.

SOLAR-POWERED "COFFEE-CAN CAR"

This model "earth-roaming" vehicle is fun to build and operate, and uses simple materials: some thin sheet aluminum; a one-pound and a half-pound coffee can (or Crisco can, well cleaned), with their plastic tops; a very small phone plug with two mating phone jacks; one of the Hankscraft gear-head motors (about 5 rpm), and a solar panel.

The half-pound coffee can both steers the model and is the vehicle's drive roller. A simple yokelike bracket to hold this drive roller is loosely bolted or pop-riveted to the main vehicle frame using rubber washers to separate roller and frame,

Above: solar powered "coffee-can car." The near roller is held in a yoke or bracket loosely bolted to the main frame. This roller contains the gear motor drive. The micro-plug right axle carries power from the L-bracket solar panel on top. The panel's power gets to the roller through a mating micro-jack and hence to the motor leads. The left axle is the motor shaft, which is attached to the left side of the yoke. The L-bracket solar panel can be swiveled in its jack in any direction to face the sun. Below: cut-away view. An Erector-Set pulley bolted on the motor shaft attaches to the yoke. Above the pulley is a metal stud (a "pop-rivet" with its shaft left "un-popped"). A straightened-out piece of the spring on this stud sticks through a hole drilled in the pulley. This keeps the pulley from turning. Thus it is the motor (with its coffee-can roller) that turns, rather than the shaft. The motor wires don't twist because the micro-plug axle is plugged into a jack in which it rotates. The jack "commutates" the power coming through the plug and jack from the solar panel to the motor.

so that the roller can be turned in any direction for steering purposes.

The gear-head motor is bulkhead-bolted inside the can to holes drilled in the metal (bottom) end of the small can so that the motor shaft "axle" sticks outside through a center hole. In operation, the motor—and the can to which it is bolted—turns, while the shaft is held firm (and prevented from turning) in a clamping bushing mounted on the yoke.

Getting power to the motor is accomplished by means of the small plug bolted to the other side of the yoke. This plug serves also as the axle for the other end of the drive roller—centered in its plastic cap. The phone-plug axle fits into the plug's mating jack which is bolted through a central hole in the plastic cap. Two insulated wires hooked to the plug extend up the yoke to another phone jack in the middle of the top surface of the vehicle frame, while two wires go between the lugs on the axle-jack in the can lid to the motor's two terminals.

Assembly must be done carefully. But once everything has been put together, and a solar panel attached and plugged into the jack on the top surface of the vehicle, power from the panel is **commutated** through the phone plug and axle-jack assembly to drive the gear-head motor—and the vehicle moves by the light of the sun.

Rubber "tires" of electrical tape, or vacuum-cleaner drive-belt "O"-rings (a hardware-store item) can be put around the drive can to make it operate on rough ground. And the lower the gear-head speed, the more powerful it is. For climbing over rough ground, use a 2 to 4 rpm gear-head motor. For faster movement on smooth surfaces, use a 5 to 8 rpm motor. (The more solar cells used, the better it will run when the sunlight is hazy.)

If the plastic can lid is too frail to hold the axle-jack, you can sandwich very thin washers—or larger aluminum disks—on each side of the plastic. Use the phone jack's bolt to hold them in place. This will stiffen the assembly.

The other—larger—coffee-can roller is held in place with a simple wire axle cut from a coat hanger. A simple bend in one end of the wire sticking out can be used to hold it to the main frame with tape.

THE SOUTH-POINTING CHINESE CARRIAGE

The south-pointing Chinese carriage is a fascinating marriage of an old idea with a new application. And a very old idea it was.

This vehicle was a full-sized wagonlike device invented by the Chinese in the first millenium, around 6000 B.C. What little has been written about it tells of its being pulled through villages. A life-sized figure stood on top of it with one arm extended. And no matter which turn in the road the carriage took, the figure always pointed in one direction—usually south. This suggests that the south-pointing Chinese carriage probably served as a sort of mechanical "compass" for groups of travelers going long distances through trackless or unfamiliar territory.

The pointing device was operated by machinery that used the movement of the carriage's two wheels to control the figure's south-pointing behavior. The differential mechanism of the modern automobile—which serves to distribute the engine's energy to the car's rear wheels, no matter where it turns—was supposed to have been invented in Europe during the late nineteenth century. However the Chinese carriage used exactly the same mechanism—only made of wood. The only other significant modern-day use of the same machinery is to control the basic direction the main cannon on a battle tank will point—no matter how rough the terrain, or how devious a route the tank takes bouncing through it.

A new use of the carriage's turning mechanism resulted in the creation of the following model. A solar generator, to be most effective, should point at the sun. Could not the figure on the carriage be replaced by a solar panel, whose power could then be used to drive a motor to power the vehicle carrying it? Then, no matter what direction the vehicle took, the panel would be kept facing the sun—and thus be able to yield its utmost power to run the vehicle.

This is a fascinating model that combines many ideas and

techniques, both ancient and ultramodern, in one very intriguing package. It stimulates thinking in an important direction—that of looking backward in time to ancient technologies that might again serve useful purposes, using modern science to improve upon them. The south-pointing Chinese carriage would make a good school project, since at school, tools for putting it together would be more readily available. A kit of its parts, plus assembly instructions, is given in the Materials List.

AN ANCIENT ENGINE, RUN ON SUNLIGHT

An example of an engine that came and went in time is the **Stirling-cycle** engine. Invented in 1816 by Robert Stirling, a Scottish minister, it would operate water pumps and the like when it was heated by a fire. A simple, slow-running, and quiet engine, it was used for many years around farms and mills, prior to the coming of the internal-combustion engines of today. The internal-combustion engine, however, must be run mostly on liquid or gaseous petroleum fuels, whose depletion is an increasing liability of these modern engines.

The Stirling-cycle engine, though slow-running, offers new promise because it can run efficiently on the heat of almost anything that will burn. This includes paper and trash—and it can run on the heat of sunlight itself, as the model shown here proves.

Model Stirling-cycle engines are cited in the Materials List. Rigged with a large Fresnel lens (or parabolic reflector), many will operate on solar heat. The details provided in the solar

The ancient south-pointing Chinese carriage in modern form. The original carriage was made of wood. This one is made of aluminum and plastic— and the figure holds the solar panel facing the sun instead of pointing south as did her ancestor. The solar pack powers the vehicle's gear motor drive.

furnace kit (also cited in the Materials List) suggest ways to tie the two concepts together into a working system.

MODEL WINDMILL TO RUN A RADIO

Wind can be harnessed to power a lot of things. Model windmill generators are not difficult to make, and when their fans turn, they will put out enough electricity to run a transistor radio—or to charge its batteries overnight for playback the next day.

A source for small model windmills—to which a small generator can be attached—is given in the Materials List. Most of the small gear-head DC motors shown in the list will also generate power when their shafts are hooked up to a windmill blade—and it turns the "motor." When using one of these gear-head motors as a generator, it is important to know the polarity—PLUS or MINUS—of its output leads, for most battery-operated radios and tape recorders must be driven with power of the proper polarity. (Used to power other models, this is not so important, for they will simply run backward if the polarity is wrong.) A 6-volt 30, 60, or 115 rpm Hankscraft motor will make a good generator. The bigger the windmill blade, the lower the gear-head motor rpm should be. If the generator will be used to recharge a radio's ni-cad batteries, a "blocking diode" will have to be put in one of the lines from the generator to the batteries. A diode is the electrical equivalent of a one-way valve in a water pipe or an aquarium pump's airline. It lets current flow in one direction,

A parabolic mirror concentrates sunlight to run a model stirling-cycle engine. To keep the engine and mirror in solar alignment a sun-tracking panel (see page 62) is attached to the rim of the reflector. Its "signal" is fed by wires to the small motor that drives a slow but powerful gear drive. This in turn swivels the mirror and motor assembly. A Fresnel lens will work with this model as well—rigged after the fashion shown for the solar furnace (pp. 55–57).

but not the other way. Without the diode, if the wind stopped blowing, energy stored in the radio batteries would "back-feed" and run the windmill generator like the motor it is, wasting the energy. The diode will prevent this.

Making your own windmill blade isn't too difficult. A 10-inch circular piece of thin aluminum should be evenly marked with twelve lines from its rim to about 1½ to 2 inches from a ⅛-inch center hole drilled through the sheet. Using a band saw, carefully slice the aluminum in from the edge along each line. When finished, there will be twelve "wedges" cut in the disc, but still attached at the center. Using pliers, gently bend each wedge about 45 to 60 degrees in one direction to create the "fan" surfaces against which the wind will push. When all the wedges have been bent into their proper shape, a little sanding will get rid of the burrs left from sawing. A coat of paint can be used to dress it up.

Mounting the blade will be a matter of what kinds of hardware fittings you can find at hardware stores or hobby shops. A small end-fitting for a shower-curtain rod will give you an idea of what kind of plate to attach to the fan blade so that a piece of ⅛-inch rod can be attached to the blade as an axle. Erector-set struts and other parts can be used to make a frame and bearings for the windmill axle—and a strut at the other end of the shaft should be bolted to the generator so its shaft is in line with that of the windmill. A spring, or hobby-shop coupler will join the two shafts together. Lastly, a large tail blade can be cut from aluminum to be attached behind the generator on the frame holding both generator and windmill blade. A pipe, or more erector set parts, can be used for a tower.

Since the windmill needs to be free to turn in any direction in the wind, here is another place where a phone plug—this time a large ¼-inch plug—can be used to commutate the generator's output from the windmill to the radio, through a mating phone jack at the top of the "tower." The phone plug can swivel in the tower-mounted phone jack, from which wires go to the radio.

The radio is powered from the model windmill-generator.

HAND GENERATORS (THEY RUN ON YOUR ENERGY)

In the picture on page 53 the "coffee-can car" is run by the use of a little hand-crank generator. What has this to do with solar energy? Well, where do you get the energy to crank the generator? From food, of course. And if you trace it back—the meat, cereal, or vegetables—it all was grown by sunlight. Many of today's battery-operated products—small radios and tape recorders, and many motorized toys and models—will operate on the energy of a hand-cranked generator, suitably wired, that plugs into the devices. A DC hand generator is listed in the Materials List; it can be plugged into radios and a number of the models described earlier—once the generator's line cord has been fitted with a small phone plug to fit them. (But watch which way you turn the crank, when playing a radio with the generator. It's polarity will reverse when you crank in the opposite direction.) Many small hand-generator flashlights are sold today that can, with care, be wired to run these things. Some put out AC (alternating) current, but a small full-wave rectifier from an electronics or hobby store can convert the output to DC current (and serve to block back-flow of the current, if you use it to charge radio batteries). Your school science teacher or another student knowledgeable about electrical hookups can help you with the wiring.

The kinds of projects described above are the most effective way to get acquainted with the growing world of solar energy. And they will stimulate ideas for useful solar energy products that should grow out of your increased understanding of the subject. Each model you build and test will better acquaint you with the great potential of solar energy to serve our energy needs more fully than ever before. And each model will help you appreciate just how much energy there is in sunlight, if we will just use it.

A hand generator (included in Materials List) is used to run the coffee-can car (see page 64).

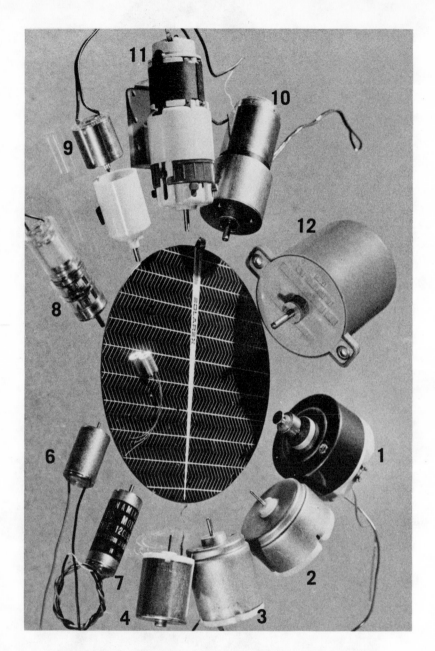

Motors that run on solar cells. The array shown includes
fine instrument-grade motors, as well as low-drain and
lower-cost "commercial" grade motors that will operate
well on the output of a few solar cells. (The numbers
refer to items on the Materials List.)

MATERIALS LIST

Item	Page & code	Description	Comment	Price	Catalog Model no.	Source
Solar cells (not shown)		Various sizes; single & shingled round, square & wedges	For making your own lashups. Low-cost surplus, in varying inventory	varies, obtain in catalog	obtain in catalog	Herbach & Rademan 401 East Erie St. Philadelphia, Pa. 19134 or Poly Paks Box 942 South Lynnfield, Mass. 01940
Solar cell	Pg 33 (center)	4" large cell	High current, with leads for easy hookup	$30	42,314	Edmund Scientific Barrington, N.J. 08007
Solar panel	Pg 33 (top)	Plastic encased sealed panel for outdoor use. 5 large cells	Stirling-cycle engine ni-cad cells and powering high-drain needs	$60	S5-200	Herbach & Rademan

Item	Page	Description	Details	Price	Model	Supplier
Solar panel	Pg 33 (lower right)	Plastic cased with kit for attaching to radio, etc.	Comes with leads for attaching your own plug. 4.5 and 6 v. models	$15	HSB4.5 (v.) HSB6 (v.)	Optical Coating Labs, Inc., 15251 East Julian Rd. City of Industry, Calif. 91746
"	Pg 33 (left)	Glass and metal sealed for use outdoors	All weather, for charging 12 v. storage cells	$100	CSP16.5 v.	Optical Coating Labs, Inc. (see above)
Solar panel (not shown)		Panel to charge 12 v. storage batteries	As above, but higher current	$400	Catalog 72,125	Edmund Scientific
Solar panel (not shown)		Thin film cadmium-sulphide solar generator. Packaged for outdoor use	Used to charge 12 v. storage batteries on boats. Printed-circuit technology employed	$100	SES "Onboard" solar power	SES, Inc. One Tralee Industrial Park, Newark, Del. 19711
Solar demon-strators	Pg 24 left	Propeller; with shingled cells	Update of first marketed in 1950s	$20	X-200	Optical Coating Labs
"	Pg 24 middle	Propeller; with ¼-round cells		$20	(solar fan cube)	The Ecology Shop 1520 Gridley Lane Silver Spring, Md. 20902

Solar demonstrators	Pg 24	(Similar; not shown)	Larger cells	$20	42,287	Edmund Scientific
"	"	"	Same, but with taps for external hookup of motors, etc.	$50 etc.	72,126	"
"	Pg 24 right	Checkered disc, shingled cells	Totally enclosed, no external parts	$15	Q5293-X	Herbach & Rademan
Solar motor	Pg 76 (no. 1)	Straight shaft permanent-magnet motors in various sizes and rpm's	Low-cost commercial grade motors with low-drain features	$2	TM20K150	"
"	Pg 76 (no. 2)	"	"	$4	GO 56#1	Aristo-Craft 314 Fifth Avenue New York, N.Y. 10001
"	Pg 76 (no. 3)	"	"	$4	F148-B#3	"
"	Pg 76 (no. 4)	"	"	$4	RM120 07800 /911466	"
"	Pg 76 (no. 9)	Portescap: type 16C. Similar to pictured motor	Very low-drain instrument grade motors. For long-lived, applications. (Current motors screw to gearbox)	Motor alone: $20.33 Gearbox: $18.83	Motor alone: 3P40ME1804 Gearbox: 3G40ME186D	Stock Drive Products 55 S. Denton Ave. New Hyde Park, N.Y. 11040

Item	Page & code	Description	Comment	Price	Catalog Model no.	Source
Solar motors	Pg 76 (no. 10)	Portescap gear head; motor model 22C11–213–5, with B26–8:1 gearbox	Motor-gear box assembly	$29 $45	Motor alone: 3P41MB32H7 With gearbox: 3G43MB0008	"
"	Pg 76 (no. 6)	Namiki: straight shaft		$27; 2 @ $18 each	12CL-2001	Namiki Precision Jewel Co., Ltd. Suite 8905 1 World Trade Center New York, N.Y. 10048
"	Pg 76 (no. 7)	Namiki: straight shaft; for more power		$30; 2 @ $19 each	12CL-3001	"
"	Pg 76 (no. 8)	Above, with gearbox. Many ratios available	(Plastic-cased demonstrator. Sold in metal only)		(Obtain catalog)	"
"	Pg 76 (no. 11)	Mico perm. mini-Richard, multi-rpm gearmotor	"Gear-shift" for rpm's from 3:1 to 60:1. High drain	$18	(Marx-Luder)	Aristo-Craft

Item	Page	Description	Notes	Price	Model/No.	Source
Solar motor	Pg 76 (no. 12)	Hankscraft bulk-head-mounting display motors 13 ratios; from .5 to 115 rpm, in 3, 6, and 12 v.	Very low drain. Soldering to motor leads must be done carefully so as not to melt plastic case. Use heat sink or clip solar leads to motor	$8	3216-00 + rpm & volts	Stock Drive (some rpm's also available from Edmund Scientific)
Lens	Pg 56 (top)	Solar Furnace Kit with Fresnel lens instructions, data & experiments		$6	70,533	Edmund Scientific
" (not shown)		Larger square Fresnel lens to run Stirling-cycle engine	By using solar furnace approach, Stirling-cycle engine can run on sunlight	$10	60,500	"
Lens	Pg 70	18" parabolic mirror for solar drive of heat engines	Can be used instead of fresnel lens to solar power Stirling-cycle engine	$12	80,254	"
Stirling-cycle engines (not shown)		Alcohol-burning working model Stirling-cycle engine	Can be adapted to solar operation using above-listed lenses	$40	Model 1000	ECO-Motor Industries Ltd. P.O. Box 934 Guelph, N1H 6M6 Ontario, Canada

Type	Page	Name	Description	Price	Model	Supplier
Stirling-cycle engines (not shown)		Swash-plate Stirling engine	Modern-version of stirling concepts	$40	Model 2000	"
"		Ericsson design Stirling engine. Castings kit	Requires shop lathe & tools to machine with instructions	$20	Model 3000	"
Model	Pg 68	South-Pointing Chinese Chariot kit	Solar-driven historical mechanical orienting device. Kit of parts & instructions	$15	CK 118	Stock Drive
Hand Generator (not shown)		AC Hand-generator flashlight	Can be fitted with micro-jack to bi-pass light for external power use. Requires full-wave rectifier for DC current output	$8	"Flashbright"	(A Janex Prod.; in toy shops)
"		"	"	$15	61,086	Edmund Scientific
Hand Generator	Pg 53	DC Hand generator for operating models, radios, tape recorders	Output can be used directly, with proper crank direction for desired polarity	$6	"Genecon"	Aristo-Craft

Item	Page	Description	Function	Price	Number	Supplier
Solar flashlight	Pg 27	Solarex flashlight with plug-in solar panel	Sunlight recharges batteries for night use	$30	61,102	Edmund Scientific, and The Ecology Shop
Windmills (not shown)		12″-blade model windmill	Suitable for use with 30–115 rpm Hankscraft gear motor to make wind generator	$35	71,924	Edmund Scientific
Plug & jack	Pg 65 (bottom, at left)	Switchcraft-made micro-plug & jack	Used to make axle commutator & solar plug-in modules & other power hookups	50¢ each	Plug: #850 Jack: TR-2A	(From electronics parts suppliers)
Stirling engine (not shown)		Model of the Henrique Stirling engine.	Comes with book by Andy Ross on Stirling cycle engines.	$27 (Book alone, $4)		Solar Engines 2937 West Indian School Road Phoenix, Ariz. 85017

The Materials List is to aid your finding specialized items that have been mentioned in this book. The suppliers of these items offer many other related kits, models, and devices that may be of interest to you, and so you should request catalogs from those who provide them. The prices given are rounded figures that were valid as of the book's publication date. They are, of course, subject to change and are placed here only to give you some idea of the range of costs that these solar materials cover. Many of the items are ready to operate, but many are kits of parts and materials that you must assemble or prepare. Before obtaining such kits, be sure you have the tools, skills, and the will, to carry out their instructions.

GLOSSARY

Amperage: A measure of the volume of flow of an electrical current.

Calorie: The amount of heat required to raise the temperature of one gram of water one degree celsius.

Chlorophyll: The green coloring matter of plants that in the presence of light plays a role in the conversion of water, carbon dioxide, and other inorganic matter into the carbohydrate material of plant life.

Commutator: A set of electrical contacts that can convey electrical current between stationary and rotating devices.

Convected heat: Transmittable heat derived from the absorption of radiant energy (sunlight) by darkened materials of solar collectors.

Current: The flow of electricity, comparable to the flow of a stream of water.

Direct conversion: The immediate utilization of sunlight as it falls—it is converted directly to heat or electrical energy.

Efficiency: See Efficiency of conversion.

Efficiency of conversion: The amount of actual energy derived, by any technique, in relation to the total quantity of energy existing in any source being tapped; expressed as a percentage.

Heat exchanger: A device like a car radiator for moving heat between two isolated mediums (such as air or liquid working-fluids) without mixing the mediums themselves.

Hydroelectric: Producing electrical power by the extraction of energy from the force of moving (usually falling) water.

Indirect conversion: The indirect utilization of solar energy from such sources as solar-produced winds, thermal currents in air and water, and wave action.

Langley: The amount of energy from solar radiation that, falling on an area of one square centimeter facing the sun on a clear day, equals one calorie of heat.

Parabolic reflector: A bowl- or cylinder-shaped mirror that reflects light from a given source (such as the sun), falling anywhere on the mirror's surface, to a concentrated common focal point.

Photoelectric: Pertaining to electric effects produced by light.

Photosynthesis: The formation of the carbohydrate living matter of plant life from water, carbon dioxide, and other inorganic matter, by the interaction of sunlight and chlorophyll.

Photovoltaic: Providing a source of electric current under the influence of light.

Photovoltaic generation: Direct and continuous generation of electrical energy by a material whenever it is illuminated by light; this is accomplished without breakdown of the material.

Polarity: The condition of being positive or negative in the electrical flow of current in an electrical circuit.

Redundancy: The incorporation of exact duplications of systems or devices that can be made to perform the services of their counterparts should they fail to operate or require periodic rest periods.

Silicon cells: Photovoltaic generators whose base material is made of silicon.

Solar cells: Photovoltaic generators that yield electrical current when exposed to certain wavelengths of light.

Solar insolation: The radiant energy from sunlight received by a given area of earth; the rate of such radiant energy per given unit measure of exposed surface.

Stirling-cycle: The cyclical heat-exchange function in the working fluid (usually an inert gas) of an engine that derives its motive force from the heating of its working fluid.

Thermal convection: The transfer of heat in a liquid body causing the less-dense, higher-temperature liquid to rise in a system.

Thermal gradient: The range of temperature (heat) difference at different levels of depth in a volume of matter (usually lakes and ocean-water bodies).

Thermal syphoning: The rising flow of less-dense, higher-temperature liquids in the plumbing system. Usually associated with solar heat collection and storage.

Torque: A turning or twisting force; rotary effort.

Voltage: A measure of the force of an electric current.

Working fluid: The liquid or gas in a heat collection system (or engine) that transfers heat throughout the system.

READING LIST

Anderson, Bryce. THE SOLAR HOME BOOK. Edited by Michael Riordan and Linda Goodman. Harrisville, N.H.: Cheshire Books, 1976

Behrman, Daniel. SOLAR ENERGY: THE AWAKENING SCIENCE. Boston: Little, Brown & Co., 1976

Branley, Franklyn M. ENERGY FOR THE 21ST CENTURY. New York: Thomas Y. Crowell, 1975

Brinkworth, B. J. SOLAR ENERGY FOR MAN. New York: John Wiley & Sons, 1972

Carr, Donald. ENERGY AND THE EARTH MACHINE. New York: Norton, 1976

Clark, Wilson. ENERGY FOR SURVIVAL. New York: Doubleday, 1975. Paperback

Halacy, D. S. Jr. THE COMING OF SOLAR ENERGY. New York: Harper & Row, 1973. Also available in paperback. Avon Books

————. SOLAR SCIENCE PROJECTS FOR A CLEANER ENVIRONMENT. New York: Scholastic Books Services, 1974

Marshall, James. GOING, GOING, GONE? New York: Coward McCann, Geoghegan, Inc., 1976

Thomason, Harry E., and Harry J. L. Thomason, Jr. SOLAR GREENHOUSE AND SWIMMING POOL. Barrington, New Jersey: Edmund Scientific Co., 1974

————. SOLAR HOUSE HEATING AND AIR-CONDITIONING SYSTEMS. Barrington, New Jersey: Edmund Scientific Co., 1973

————. SOLAR HOUSES AND SOLAR HOUSE MODELS. Barrington, New Jersey: Edmund Scientific Co., 1976

For current articles on solar energy consult the READERS' GUIDE TO PERIODICAL LITERATURE in your library. Under the heading "Solar Energy" you will find listed articles from such magazines as ENVIRONMENT, FORTUNE, POPULAR SCIENCE, SCIENTIFIC AMERICAN, and SMITHSONIAN.

INDEX

Gear-head motor, 58–61, 64, 66, 69, 71

Generators
    hand, 74, 82
    hydroelectric, 23
    solar, 58–61
    wind, 39, 71

Glaubers salts, 37
Glycol, 33
Greeks, 2

Hand generators, 74, 82
Hankscraft motor, 61, 64, 71
Heat collectors, 31, 32
Heat exchanger, 33, 34
Heating systems, hot-air, 32, 34
Holland, 39
Hot-air engine, 8
Hot-air heating system, 32, 34
Houses, solar-heated, 37–38
Hurricanes, 41
Hydroelectric generators, 23
Hydroelectric power, 1, 30, 42

Indirect conversion, 30, 39
Ingots, silicon, 15, 45
Insulation, 35–36
Internal-combustion engine, 69
Irrigation, 2
Irrigation pumps, 50

Kelp, 25

Langley, Samuel, 22
Langley, unit of measurement, 22, 23
Lavoisier, Antoine, 2
Lenses, 57, 69, 81
Light meters, 8
Light, strength of, 8–9
Lightbaffle, 61
Liquid systems, 32

Massachusetts Institute of Technology, 37
Materials, listed, 77–83
Microwave power, 49
Mining, 29
Mirrors, computer controlled, 51
Motorized toys, 74

Motors
    gear-head, 58–61, 64, 66, 69, 71
    Hankscraft, 61, 64, 71
    portescap, 61
    shaft, straight-output, 60
    solar, 58–61, 79–81

Namiki gear-head motor, 61
National Aeronautics and Space Administration, 41, 52
Nuclear energy, 29
Nuclear reactors, 29
Nuclear wastes, 29

Oil, 2, 29
Organic materials, converted to fuel, 52
Organic matter, and electricity, 51
Oxyacetylene torch, 57

Paper, 52
Parabolic reflections, 2, 50
Parallel hookup, 13
Photoelectric cell, 8
Photons, 10, 22
Photosynthesis, 25, 51, 52–54
Photovoltaic cell, 8
Photovoltaic collector, 49
Photovoltaic generation, 45, 46
Plants, 1
    growth rate, 54
Plastics, 26
Polarity, 61
Pollution, 26, 52
Population growth, 1
Portescap motor, 61
Printed-circuit solar cells, 46
Printed circuits, 46

Radios, 74
Rectifier, 74
Redundancy, 21, 85
Refrigeration, 35
Reservoirs, 42
Romans, 2
Rotors, 41

Sahara desert, 22